LET'S RIDE A
BIKE

WRITTEN & ILLUSTRATED BY
RUTH WALTON

SEA-TO-SEA

Mankato Collingwood London

When it's good weather, we ride our bikes to school.
We get there much quicker than when we walk!

Riding a bike helps keep you physically fit and
healthy. It is also a very safe way to travel,
as long as you are careful and remember that
other people use the road and sidewalk, too.

4

Around the world, millions of people ride their bikes every day for lots of different reasons.

What other reasons can you think of to ride a bike?

CYCLING FOR WORK

All over the world, people use bikes to help with **deliveries,** because they are fast and good for carrying heavy loads.

A fruit seller in Vietnam.

Police officers use bikes to get through crowds and narrow streets.

A police officer in Canada.

A postal worker in England.

Bikes are great for delivering the mail around towns and cities.

6

CYCLING FOR FUN

Riding a bike can be really fun! There are many different kinds of bike to use for having fun.

This BMX bike rider is doing a trick!

Mountain biking in the desert.

BMX bikes are good for doing **stunts**. Mountain bikes are great for exploring the countryside and racing bikes go fast on roads.

Racing bikes can go really fast!

Do you have a bike?

What do you like to use it for?

Do You Know How a Bike Works?

When you press your foot down on the **pedal** of a bike, it turns the front **sprocket**.

The **chain** is wrapped around the front and rear sprocket. When the chain moves, it makes the wheels turn around.

Some bikes have **gears**, which help you ride at different speeds and get up hills more easily.

All bikes should have **brakes** to help them slow down and stop. The brakes work by pressing onto the **wheel rims** to stop them from turning.

Which of these parts can you find on the diagram?

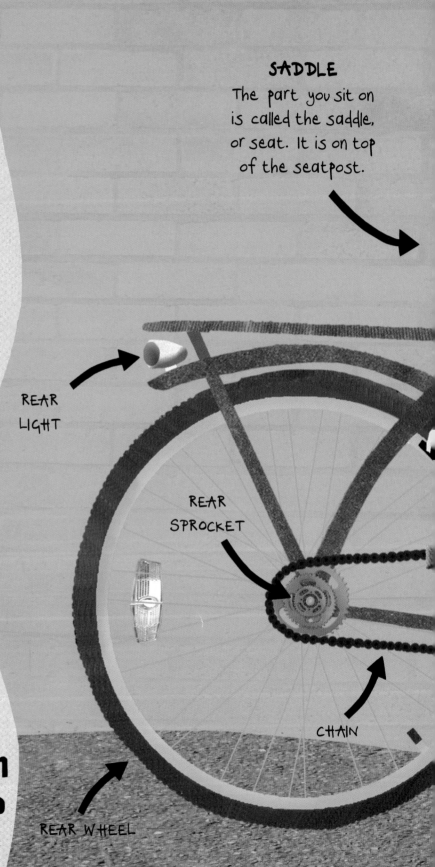

SADDLE
The part you sit on is called the saddle, or seat. It is on top of the seatpost.

REAR LIGHT

REAR SPROCKET

CHAIN

REAR WHEEL

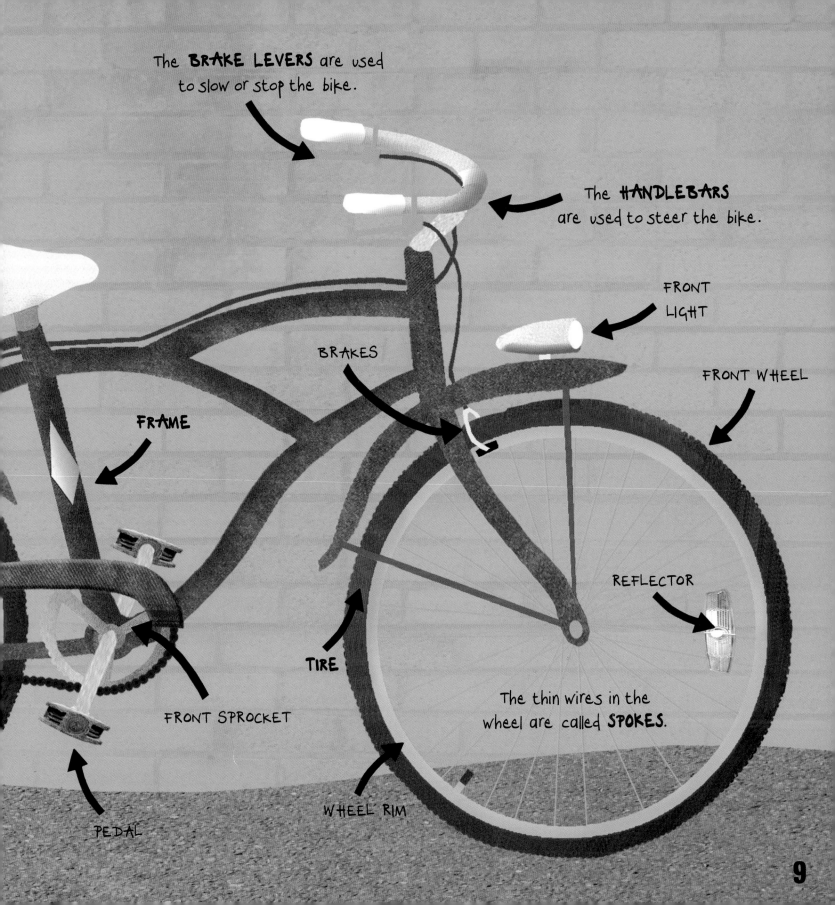

The **BRAKE LEVERS** are used to slow or stop the bike.

The **HANDLEBARS** are used to steer the bike.

FRONT LIGHT

BRAKES

FRONT WHEEL

FRAME

TIRE

REFLECTOR

FRONT SPROCKET

The thin wires in the wheel are called **SPOKES**.

WHEEL RIM

PEDAL

9

WHEN WERE BICYCLES INVENTED?

1817 The first ever bike was called a draisine. It was made out of wood and it didn't have any pedals.

1860s The first bike with pedals was called a velocipede. The wooden frame had metal tires. It rattled a lot so people called it the bone-shaker!

1870s This bike is called a pennyfarthing. The front wheel is much larger than the back wheel, which helps it to go faster without needing a chain.

1890s Bicycle chains, brakes, and air-filled tires were invented, making cycling much easier and safer. This kind of bike is called a safety bike.

1920s Child-sized bicycles are made for the first time, and riding a bike becomes a common hobby for children.

There are lots of different kinds of bike available to choose from today. Many bikes are made from steel.

Do you know where steel comes from?

Steel is an **alloy** made from a type of metal called iron. Iron is made from **iron ore**, which is mined from the earth using excavators.

This is iron ore.

The iron ore is loaded onto trucks and taken to the **foundry.** The ore is heated to **extract** the iron.

When the iron gets very hot, it turns into liquid. The liquid iron is blended with other **minerals** and it becomes steel.

Liquid steel can be made into many different shapes. When it cools, it is strong and it doesn't **rust** easily. All of these **properties** of steel make it perfect for making bike frames!

The foundry is a big factory.

It's very hot in the foundry.

13

How Is a Bike Frame Made?

Bike frames are made from steel tubes because they are strong and light.

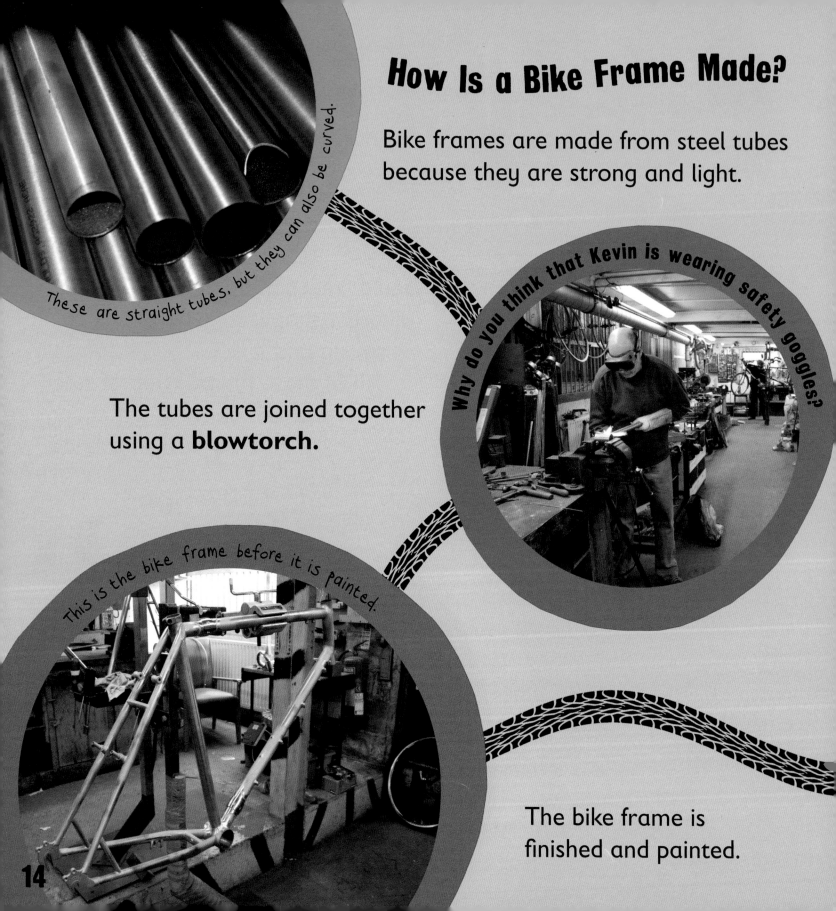

These are straight tubes, but they can also be curved.

The tubes are joined together using a **blowtorch.**

Why do you think that Kevin is wearing safety goggles?

This is the bike frame before it is painted.

The bike frame is finished and painted.

The frame is taken to the workshop and many extra parts are added.

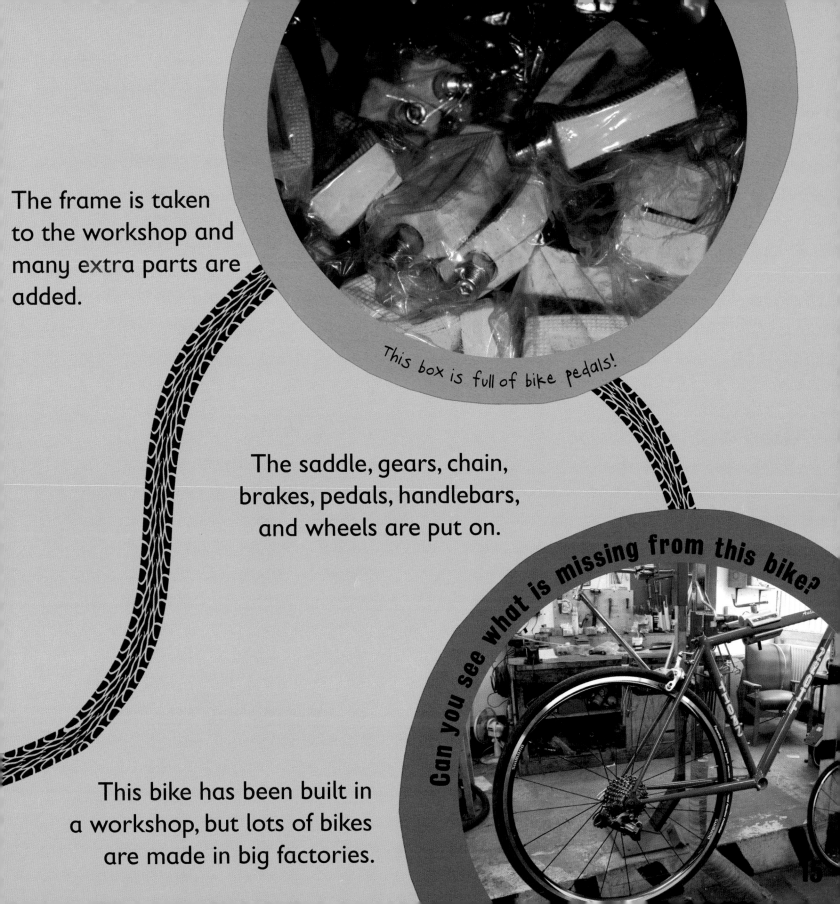

This box is full of bike pedals!

The saddle, gears, chain, brakes, pedals, handlebars, and wheels are put on.

Can you see what is missing from this bike?

This bike has been built in a workshop, but lots of bikes are made in big factories.

17

All bike wheels today are fitted with tires. Most tires are made from a material called **rubber,** which is made from **latex** mixed with chemicals, fabric, and oil.

Latex drips from the tree into a bowl.

Latex comes from the **sap** of the rubber tree, which grows in hot countries.

Raised patterns help tires grip the road better!

This is the air **valve**, where you can attach a pump to add more air!

If your tire is flat, you might have a **puncture**. It is easy to learn how to fix a flat tire!

Inside each bike tire is an **inner tube**, which is filled with air. This helps stop it feeling bumpy when you ride!

Have you ever fixed a flat tire?

Staying Safe On Your Bike!

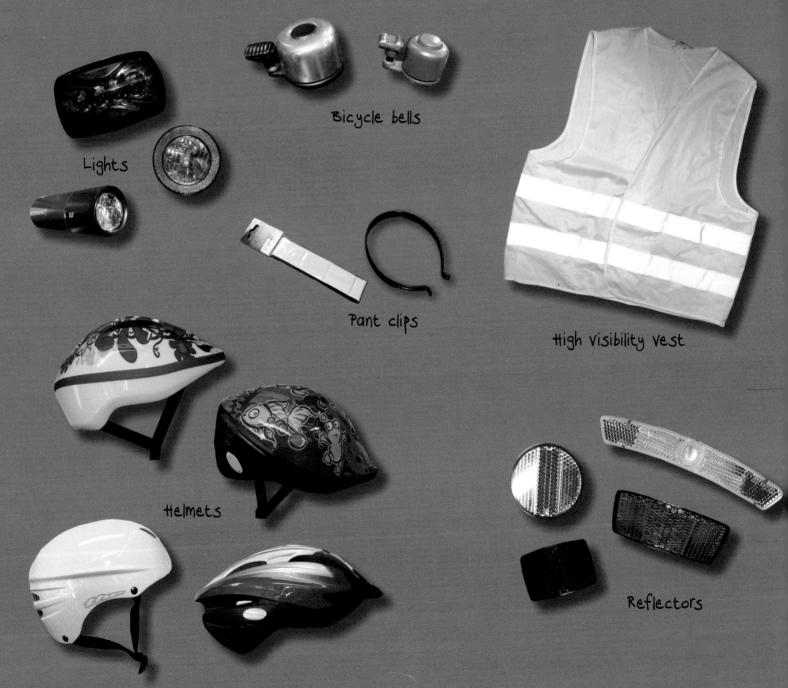

Lights

Bicycle bells

High Visibility Vest

Pant clips

Helmets

Reflectors

All of these things will help you to be safe when riding your bike.

How do you think each item helps keep you safe?

Make sure your tires are pumped up. It makes riding your bike much easier!

Check that your seat is at the right height for you. Your leg should be nearly straight when the pedal is at its lowest point.

It is good to check that your brakes work before you go for a bike ride.

Make sure that you are wearing your helmet properly, or it won't protect you if you fall!

This is how it should look!

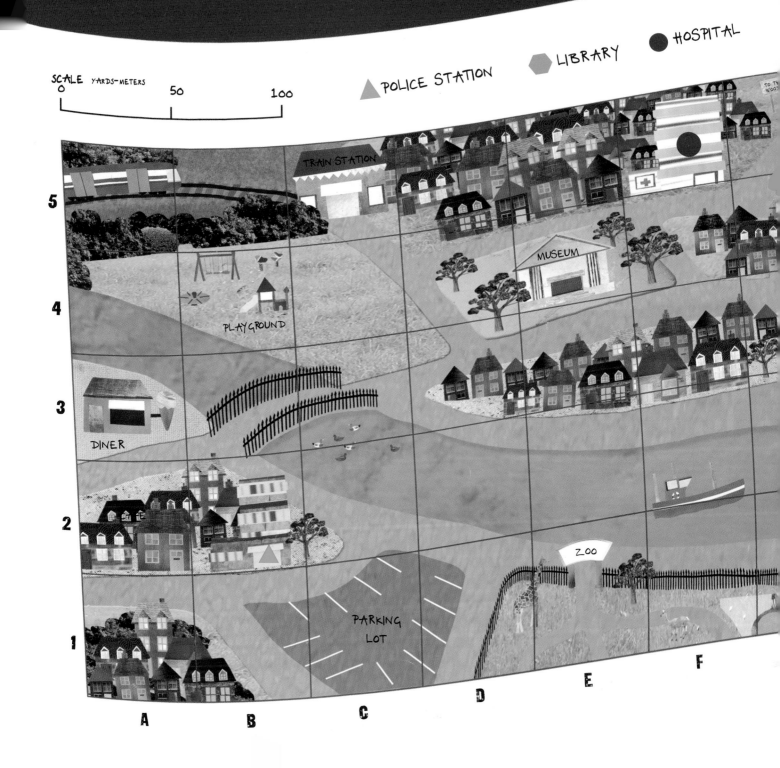

ore you set off on a bike ride, it can be fun to use
ap to plan your route...

SCALE YARDS—METERS
0   50   100

POLICE STATION
LIBRARY
HOSPITAL

TRAIN STATION

MUSEUM

PLAYGROUND

DINER

ZOO

PARKING LOT

A   B   C   D   E   F

5

4

3

2

1

CASTLE

SCHOOL

TO THE BEACH

H   i   J

Where do you want to go?

HOW TO USE A MAP

This map has a **grid** to help you find what you are looking for.

The **grid reference** for the museum is E4.

What are the grid references for the castle and the zoo?

Most maps have **symbols** to help you find things quickly.

The symbol for the hospital is a red circle.

What is the symbol for the police station and what is its grid reference?

Going for a bike ride is great for keeping you healthy, but riding up hills can be hard!

If your bike has gears it can make it much easier. Try changing into a low gear before you start riding up a hill.

How Do Bicycle Gears Work?

The bike chain is connected to a series of sprockets, which are different sizes. When you move the gear lever, it shifts the chain from one sprocket to the next. If the chain is on a small sprocket, the pedals will be easier to turn. This is called a low gear. When the chain is on a larger sprocket, the pedals will be harder to turn. This is called a high gear.

Why do you think it is easier to ride downhill?

Always test your brakes before going down a hill.

What Is Gravity?

Gravity is an invisible **force** that pulls objects together. Every planet has its own gravity that pulls objects toward its center. The Earth's gravity is what makes objects fall to the ground when you drop them, and what keeps us from drifting off into space!

When you ride your bike on a hill, gravity is pulling you downward. So gravity is why it is harder to ride up hills and easier to ride down them.

Riding down hills is lots of fun because gravity helps you go faster without pedaling. Remember to keep your hands on the brakes so you can slow down or stop if you need to!

Where are you going to ride your bike today?

ACTIVITY:
Design a Bike!

Here are a few things that you might need to make your own bike design...

Eraser

Pencil crayons

Letter paper

Pencil sharpener

Ruler

Pencil

Look at these pictures and answer the questions to get some ideas.

How tall will it be?

How many wheels will it have?

Will it take passengers?

Will it go on land or water?

Where will you sit?

Will it have a trailer?

What will the handlebars look like?

How many people can ride it?

Don't worry about your drawing, just go wild
and think of what the coolest bike in the world would look like...

Use your imagination to design the bike of your dreams!

Glossary

Alloy a mixture of metals

Blowtorch a tool that uses heat from a gas flame to join pieces of metal

Brake levers levers on handlebars that operate the brakes

Brakes the part of the bike that presses against the wheel rim to slow the bike down, or bring it to a stop

Chain a line of connected links of metal

Deliveries the transportation of goods from place to place

Extract take something out

Force strength or power

Foundry a factory where steel is made

Frame the metal structure of a bike

Gears the gears move the bike chain onto a bigger or smaller sprocket. This allows the cyclist to change speed or go up hills more easily

Grid a network of squares on a map

Grid reference numbers and letters used to pinpoint a part of a map

Handlebars a bar with a handle at each end, used to steer a bike

Healthy fit and well

Inner tube tube of rubber, filled with air, inside the bike tire

Iron ore a material containing iron, found in rocks

Latex a milky liquid made by rubber trees

Minerals nonliving substances that occur naturally in the ground

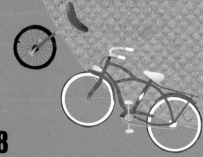

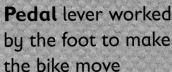

Pedal lever worked by the foot to make the bike move

Properties special qualities, such as strength

Puncture small hole in a tire, allowing the air to escape

Rubber a material made from the latex produced by rubber trees, or by mixing oil and chemicals together

Rust a reddish-brown coating that forms on some metals when they are exposed to air and water

Saddle the seat of a bike

Sap the liquid in plants. It carries food supplies around the plant

Spokes the wires that connect the center of the wheel to the wheel rim

Sprocket a wheel with jagged teeth that connect with the links in a bike chain

Stunt a daring action performed to attract attention

Symbol a sign that represents something

Tire the rubber structure around a wheel, protecting the inner tube

Valve a device for controlling the flow of air in one direction. It prevents air from escaping from the tire and is used to pass air into the tire

Wheel rim the outer edge of a metal wheel

Index

This edition first published in 2013 by
Sea-to-Sea Publications
Distributed by Black Rabbit Books
P.O. Box 3263, Mankato, Minnesota 56002

Text and illustrations copyright
© Ruth Walton 2009, 2013

Printed in the United States of America, North
Mankato, MN.

All rights reserved.

9 8 7 6 5 4 3 2

Published by arrangement with the
Watts Publishing Group Ltd., London.

Library of Congress Cataloging-in-Publication Data

Walton, Ruth.
  Let's ride a bike / written & illustrated by Ruth
Walton.
    p. cm. -- (Let's find out)
  Includes index.
  Summary: "Discusses uses of bicycles, how bikes are
made and designed, and bicycle safety and riding
tips"-- Provided by publisher.
  ISBN 978-1-59771-385-6 (alk. paper)
  1. Bicycles--Juvenile literature. 2. Cycling--Juvenile
literature. I. Title.
  TL412.W35 2013
  629.28'472--dc23

2011052691

Series Editor: Sarah Peutrill
Art Director: Jonathan Hair

Photographs: Ruth Walton, unless otherwise credited.

Picture credits: I Stock Photo: 6t (Jakob Leitner), 7t
(James Ferrie), 7b (Dieter Spears), 12 (background:
Ricardo Azoury), 13t (GoosePhotographic), 13b
(Muzaffer Topuz), 16m (yuliang11), 17b (Arthur
Carlo Franco), 19b (Michael Flippo), 26t (Sean
Warren), 26m (Klaus Nilkens), 26b (Ken Graff), 27tl
(Mark Jensen), 27tr (Georg Hafner), 27m (Timothy
Large), 27bl (luxxtek), 27br (Ferran Traite Soler).
Shutterstock: 6m, 7m (Geir Olav Lyngfjell).
Every attempt has been made to clear copyright.
Should there be any inadvertent omission please
apply to the publisher for rectification.

RD/6000006415/001
May 2012